Wine Tasting

Guide

A Beginner's Wine Tasting Guide to
Understanding Wine, Picking the Right Glass for
the Right Wine, Pouring and Serving Wine and
Hosting the Best Wine Tasting Party Around

By Bruno Gordon

Contents

Thank you for buying this book and I hope that you will find it useful. If you will want to share your thoughts on this book, you can do so by leaving a review on the Amazon page, it helps me out a lot.

Introduction

Wine tasting is seen as a classy past time for plenty of individuals. Before you start wine tasting, there are lots of things you need to learn about wine. To some individuals, wine tasting is a skill.

Understanding wine is simple. There are lots of kinds of wine and it is made all over the globe in various regions. Wine tasting calls for knowledge of the kinds of wine. It is necessary to understand which kinds of glasses to pick for various wines and how to clean them. It is additionally crucial to understand how to pour and offer wine appropriately. Wine tasting entails numerous things. The aim of this book is to present you to all you have to understand about wine so you can start wine tasting with your buddies.

Chapter 1: About Wine

Wine is a drink fermented from grape juice consisting of alcohol. Grapes have a natural chemical balance, and that enables them to ferment without the requirement to include any sugars, enzymes, acid, or any other kinds of nutrients to the components.

When wine is made, grapes are squashed utilizing various kinds of yeast. The yeast consumes the natural sugars discovered in grapes. This consumption changes the grapes into alcohol. Based upon the kinds of wine made, numerous grape varieties are utilized to make wine.

Evidence reveals that the earliest creations of wine happened as early as 6000 BC in locations such as Georgia, Israel, and Iran. Certain archaeologists state that as early as 7000 BC, grapes were combined with rice to create other kinds of fermented beverages in China. This is seen as the precursor of rice wine.

In Europe, wine goes back to as early as 4000 BC in a few of the archaeological sites situated in Greece. These identical sites consist of the earliest proof in the world of grapes being squashed. Ancient Egypt has a documented history of wine being utilized ceremonially. Places such as the Roman Catholic Church deemed wine essential to celebrate Mass. In France, the monks created wine for many years and kept it in caves underneath.

Throughout the Islamic Golden Age, the wine was prohibited up until the appearance of the distilling techniques, and that led it to be accepted and legalized for cosmetic and medical usages only. There were numerous recipes created with wine throughout this time.

Grape Varieties

Wine is created from several grape varieties. The Vitis vinifera is the primary grape. This grape is described by law as having a minimum of 75% to 85%. The outcome stemming from these kinds of grapes is a varietal. This kind of wine is known to individuals as Chardonnay, the Pinot Noir or Merlot. The locations of the globe where these grapes are cultivated consist of regions such as Bordeaux and Rhone Valley.

Wines are not constantly produced from the identical species of grapes. They might be from the identical vintage but of various species. When 2 species of grapes are crossed, it is referred to as a hybrid. The Concord grape is a hybrid grape originating from various grape species like the Vitis labrusca, Vitis aestivalis, Vitis rupestris, Vitis rotundiafolia and Vitis riparia. These grapes are mostly cultivated in North America for standard use. There are numerous foods created from these grapes that consist of things such as jam, jelly, grape juice, and even in some cases, wine.

Classifications

Wine is usually categorized based upon the various parts of the globe. There are policies which govern how wine is categorized. For instance, in Europe, wine is categorized by the region it originates from. If it originates from Chianti or Bordeaux, the wine is categorized as this.

Nations that are not European do not categorize their wines by the various regions the wine is made. They categorize the wine based upon the kind of grapes utilized to create the wine. Wines categorized by the various grape types consist of the Pinot Noir and the Merlot.

Certain parts of the world and wine valleys have actually acknowledged the category policies put to standard in Europe. Wine is being acknowledged regularly by the locale instead of being acknowledged by the grape. Certain wines acknowledged by the place of the vineyard and not by the grape variety consist of wines such as Australia, Napa Valley, Barrosa Valley, Willamette Valley, and Marlborough.

There have actually been efforts by wine valley regions all over the globe which are non-European to categorize wines by the wine quality. Nevertheless, these efforts have actually stopped working and have been short-lived.

Vintage

The vintage wines are wines particularly cultivated in a specific year. These wines are classified by the year in which they were cultivated instead of being classified by the various region or grape utilized to create the wine. These grapes are normally all cultivated in the identical year as well. Each year the identical wine might have a distinct variation in color and somewhat in taste.

Numerous other particular distinctions when it comes to vintages consist of the nose, body, palate, and development. They are considered to enhance their taste with age when they are kept appropriately. It is extremely frequent for wine collectors to hold onto a classic wine bottle for a special event to enjoy.

Non-Vintage

Non-vintage wines are wines made from grapes and wines, not from the identical vintage. They do preserve the consistency with the taste of the wine and the other qualities. These wines frequently sell much better since they preserve the identical taste. Even in a lousy year, these wines could be mixed and created since the grapes originate from various vintages.

Chapter 2: Various Kinds Of Wine

Fruit Wines

There are numerous wines considered to be 'fruit wines.' These wines have actually gotten the name as they have components of various kinds of fruits included in them, rather than by the utilization of grapes. They generally are going to have a name describing the kind of fruit utilized to create the wine. Plum wine and apple wine are fine instances.

Nevertheless, fruit wines are not going to be called 'wine' as the word wine is appointed particularly as a beverage created with grapes. The name of the fruit needs to be before the term wine. This is to remove confusion. This additionally entails country wine, which is the Excellent Britain variation of fruit wine and a great sign that the wine is not produced from grapes.

Many individuals produce their own fruit wine. It could be produced from any kind of food which is adequately sweet. You may need to include a bit of table sugar or honey for the appropriate quantity of sucrose.

Fruit wine is not constantly created from fruits. It could be created from various plant sources which are not seen as fruits. These kinds of fruit wines are typically created from things such as dandelion, rice, flowers, and more.

Apple wine is a German fruit wine that is produced from apples. This wine is referred to as Apfelwein in Germany. This is a type of cider with an alcoholic material of 6% to 7%. Some state the taste of this wine is sour and tart. Certain North Americans enjoy a drink in the winter season referred to as apple cider. This frequently is the identical thing yet does not consist of alcoholic content. Apfelwein is typically offered by the jug instead being sold in bottles such as other wines worldwide.

Wine could be made with many berries and fruits worldwide in cooler environments. It depends upon the kinds, and the quantity of fermentable sugars included within the fruits. Certain fruits which have excessive amounts of malic and citric acid could be fermented likewise.

Fruit wines typically have to be drank at least a year after they are made. These are not wines which improve as they age due to the fermentation problems. Due to the fact that fruits frequently require added sugars to produce fruit wines, these are not the natural sugars grapes have. They do not ferment identically and frequently require that things such as nitrogen, phosphorus, and potassium are included, which just enables the taste to last for roughly a year.

There are several fruits utilized to create fruit wines. The fruits which make the ideal fruit wines are plums, elderberries, blackberries, peaches, huckleberries, pomegranates, and blackcurrants. These fruit wines look like grape wines and taste extremely similar.

Fruit wines are produced from other fruits like apricot, cherries, bananas, blueberries and pineapple guava. Wines can additionally be produced from flowers like elderberry, hibiscus, and dandelions. Veggies like potatoes, parsnip and rhubarb are additionally utilized to create fruit wines.

Rice Wines-- Starch

Rice wine is a wine notoriously referred to as sake. This is a Japanese alcoholic beverage. Rice wine is created by fermenting naturally sweet grapes, along with other fruits. Rice starch is fermented to produce rice wine. The fermentation converts the rice starch into sugars. This procedure is extremely comparable to the procedure utilized to produce beer.

There are several kinds of rice wine. These types consist of Raksi from Tibet, Tuak from Malaysia, Lihing from Sabah, and far more. Korea additionally creates an unfiltered rice wine which is referred to as snake wine.

Barley Wine

Barley wine originated in the 19th century. It, in fact, originated from the 18th-century ales brewed in November and October. This is a terminology utilized, yet it is, in fact, a beer. Nevertheless, this is as powerful as wine yet frequently misinterpreted as a wine due to the name.

Pinot Noir

Pinot Noir originates from the grape species referred to as the Vitis vinifera. These grapes are mainly for red wine. The name is French and means 'pine' and 'black.' This describes the firmly clustered pine cone-shaped, purple-colored fruit. These grapes are most typically known as originating from Burgundy France.

These grapes are hard to grow yet are recognized to generate the finest wines on the planet. This wine is additionally considered to be among the most romantic wines on the planet as well. Pinot wine has a tendency to have a light to medium body with an aroma which may remind you of raspberries, black cherries, or currants. When the grapes are utilized young, the wine is frequently a lot lighter than other red wines. Pinot Noir is additionally utilized with Chardonnay.

A number of locations all over the world recognized for making Pinot Noir consist of the United States, Australia, Italy, Moldova, Austria, Canada, New Zealand, Switzerland, England, Germany, Spain and France. There are California wine areas in the United States recognized for generating Pinot Noir that entail the Monterey County, Sonoma Coast, San Luis Obispo County and Carneros District of Napa and Sonoma.

Chardonnay

Chardonnay is a white wine created from a green-skinned grape variety. The tastes related to a Chardonnay are of oak and terroir. It is seen as a neutral wine, light in flavor. A number of locations around the globe recognized for making Chardonnay consist of Burgundy, France, Champagne, California, North America, Italy, Australia, and the New World Wine Regions.

There are lots of kinds of Chardonnay from sweet late harvest wines and dry still wines. If a Chardonnay has not undergone malolactic fermentation, the wine is going to have an apple taste. The tougher the malic acid is when it is changed through fermentation, it is going to have a more buttery taste.

The oak is additionally charred to a specific degree, and that introduces a toastiness taste. Lots of wine tasters confuse this taste with the grapes, yet it is from the oak charring. A few of the flavors which Chardonnay could taste like because of the oak charring consist of cinnamon, coconut, spice, cloves, cream, smoke, vanilla and caramel.

When Chardonnay is fermented, it additionally impacts the taste of the wine. For example, the colder the fermentation procedure is, the more fruity the wine is. These flavors consist of pineapple and mango. Certain wineries likewise utilize yeast which is particularly cultivated, and that offers the wines an aromatic quality.

Chardonnay is the toughest wine to acknowledge in a blind tasting due to the fact that there is not a unique universal quality or style which is administered to the wine directly. There are several tastes, blends, and more. Not all Chardonnays have a smoky note, as well.

Merlot

Merlot is created mostly from the Vitis vinifera types. The many wines linked with a merlot feature the Bouche, Bouchet, Petit-Cabernet, Petit-Bouchet, Vidure, Petit-Vidure, and Sauvignon Rouge. The wine origin is from the Bordeaux grape. It is additionally believed to be created from a mutated grape from Biturica. Merlot is red wine. The term is French and means numerous sorts of thrushes.

Merlot is created in Italy, France, Romania, California, Argentina, Australia, Canada, South Africa, Chile, Hungary, Croatia, and more. Merlot's role is to include softness and body. Certain blends taste sweet, and it is most typically recognized for the balanced acid levels.

Chapter 3: Production

Countries Making Wine

The list beneath shows the top 10 wine-making nations on the planet. The number beside the nation shows the number of tons of wine produced each year by every nation. The nations are noted from 1 to 10, 1 being the top producer on the planet.

1. France-- 5.3 million

2. Italy-- 4.7 million

3. Spain-- 3.6 million

4. United States-- 2.2 million

5. Argentina-- 1.5 million

6. Australia-- 1.4 million

7. China-- 1.4 million

8. South Africa-- 1.4 million

9. Chile-- 977,000

10. Germany 890,000

The greatest growers and wineries are at least 50 degrees south or north of the equator.

Chapter 4: Wine Uses

There are various uses for wine. It is not just for consumption as it is a drink with considerable worth, and it is considered to be classy. Wine is important to various cuisines, religions, and it has various health-related advantages.

There are various wines utilized for cooking. Lots of deserts have wine, like the Black Forest Cherry. Many individuals enjoy marinating meats in a wine before barbecuing or baking in the oven.

Wine has lots of religious usages. Due to the fact that wine causes a mind-altering state, the Dionysus utilized it as a sacramental entheogen. It is an essential part of Jewish laws, like Kiddush.

The Christianity religion utilizes wine additionally throughout the Eucharist. The last dinner reveals Jesus sitting with his disciples sharing bread and consuming a glass of wine. There are lots of denominations which believe in the Eucharist, consisting of the Protestants and the Roman Catholics.

Islamic law prohibits wine. Even though Iran once had a successful wine industry, it was squelched in 1979, because of the Islamic Revolution. Any kind of alcohol is strictly prohibited.

There are likewise numerous health advantages of wine. Red wine consists of a chemical referred to as resveratrol. This chemical has chemoprotective and cardioprotective impacts in the animal studies. Procyanidins are recognized to have heart benefits, and they are most typically discovered in red wines. Procyanidins suppress the procedure in the body which narrows the blood vessels.

Sulfites are in all wines because of the fermentation procedure. Certain wines have more than others. Sulfites have actually been recognized to create issues with individuals with asthma.

Wine is recognized to be healthy to consume sometimes. If you consume one glass of wine daily, it is seen as healthy for your heart. It is fine for pregnant ladies to consume a little glass of wine every day. It is recognized to be healthy for the heart and body since it offers a peaceful impact on the brain and the muscles.

Exceedingly consuming wine could result in issues and lead to health problems if it is on a consistent basis. It is not recommended to consume excessive quantities of wine because of the high alcohol quantity in the majority of wines.

Chapter 5: Glassware

Picking a Glass

When picking wine glasses, it is essential to consider a couple of things. You typically desire a big bowl on your wine glass when tasting red wines. This provides you ample space on the glass to swirl the wine and more of a surface area. These glasses ought to enable you to pour in from 10 to 20 ounces of wine. The ideal red wine glasses are oval-shaped, and they narrow somewhat at the top of the glass.

The white wine glasses ought to be a slim flute-shaped glass. This is required if you wish to delight in white wine to the very best of its taste. A white wine glass ought to be considerably tinier than the red wine glass.

How to Hold a Wine Glass

When you are tasting wine, it is still crucial to understand how to hold your wine glass appropriately. This is going to demonstrate you are properly versed and that you have correct etiquette. You ought to constantly hold the glass by the stem.

Never ever hold the wine glass by the glass bowl. Your hands are warm, and in case you hold the glass by the bowl, you are going to warm the wine. You additionally wish to make certain you do not place any fingerprints on the glass bowl, either.

Washing Wine Glasses

There are various approaches for washing wine glasses effectively. You wish to make certain you get the glass totally clean. Certain individuals like to do a rinse technique with warm water. If you select to utilize just water with your wine glasses, make certain to get all of the residual wine out of the glass prior to setting it out to dry. You could wash your wine glasses with a sponge and mild soap as well.

Certain individuals like to utilize soda to clean their glasses. This is prevalent for washing costly glasses such as crystal. Certain glasses you could wash in the dishwashing machine. It is ideal just to wash the wine glasses which have brief stems in the dishwasher. When you wash a long-stemmed glass in the dishwashing machine, the stems are typically susceptible to breaking off.

After washing wine glasses, you ought to set them out to air dry. Place the glasses on a towel and allow them to dry. You will not have tough water stains on the glasses. In case you do wash your dishes in the dishwashing machine, it is ideal to stop the dry session and take the glasses out to air dry.

Chapter 6: About Wine Tasting and the Various Ways

Tasting Order

When you have a wine tasting celebration or you taste wine with your buddies, it is really crucial to offer the wine in the suitable order. Elderly tasters are constantly served initially, regardless of what the gender is. Ladies are going to be served next. The men ought to be served after the ladies. The host is constantly served after everybody in the room gets a glass.

When you taste various wines, you additionally need to consider the order of the wines being tasted. In case you taste sweet or heavy wines prior to light wines, they might leave a taste in your mouth. This is since they have a tendency to control the taste.

A wine taster needs to taste the lighter wines initially, or their taste buds are going to be skewed for tasting other wines. The order in which wines ought to be tasted is the following: sparkling, light white, heavy white, roses, light red, heavy red, and sweet wine.

In case you have actually never tasted the wine it could be difficult to recognize if it is heavy and if it should be the first one to be tasted. You need to evaluate the wines by other attributes like the color, nose, and look.

Evaluating Qualities

When you evaluate wine, there are a couple of things to think about. The heavier and sweeter a wine it is, you are going to have the ability to notice that. This is by the swirling technique. Red wines which are heavy and sweet and are going to leave swirls on the glass, additionally referred to as 'legs.' This is why you wish to consume your red wines out of a larger bowl-shaped glass. You want to be able to

swirl the glass to evaluate the heaviness and
sweetness of the wine.

The varietal wines present a grape aroma. An
excellent taster is going to have the ability to tell the
varietal mixes by the smell of the grape. Integration
is additionally taken into consideration by a wine
taster. Integration consists of various elements like
tannin, acid, alcohol and others. These elements
need to all be in balance. The appropriate term
when a wine is in balance with these elements is
'harmonious fusion.'

When a wine's quality is evaluated, the word
expressiveness is utilized. This is when the flavors
and aromas are properly specified in the wine and
plainly projected through the taste.

Scoring Wine

There is an established system for scoring wines. It
is essential to compare the merits of various wines.
Various elements are frequently weighed when you

score wines. It is essential to understand how to score wines when tasting them with your buddies. The elements you are going to take a look at in the wine consist of the look, the smell, additionally called the nose, the taste palate, and the general wine taste.

Not all wine scoring systems are identical. Some are weighted in a different way. For instance, the look might be 20% of the score and the nose might be 40%. The wine nose being better on one wine glass might make the wine score greater. Many critics have their own favored system. It is essential to have with a system prior to getting started with wine tasting, so your tasters and you are not puzzled.

Wine Tasting Etiquette

As wine tasting is seen as a really sophisticated practice, there is a particular etiquette you need to follow. This etiquette ought to stay the identical whether you are at a wine tasting private celebration, at a vineyard, or in a restaurant.

During a wine tasting party, you ought to just invite the number of individuals that you are able to fit conveniently in the room in which you wish to have your party. A crowd might be daunting. You do not wish for any of your guests to feel like they are being hurried during glass pouring or tasting.

Constantly make certain to have bottled water nearby when you have a wine tasting. This enables your visitors to rinse their mouths out in between tasting various wines. If you have actually simply tasted a really heavy wine, you need to have water prepared for the guests. If that is not the case, then their following tasting might be tainted because of the heaviness lingering in their mouths. Additionally, water is excellent due to the fact that guests are not going to become thirsty and they have to drink something besides the wine.

During wine tasting, it is essential to supply foods for your guests. Nevertheless, you additionally wish to make certain to have food nearby which is not going to change how the wine tastes whatsoever. The ideal snacks to have nearby consist of unflavored stuff such as bread or saltless crackers.

Decanting

Certain individuals practice decanting prior to offering wine at a wine tasting. This is really controversial to various wine aficionados. Decanting is the procedure of allowing the wine to breathe prior to offering it.

Certain individuals allow their wine to breathe for a couple of hours prior to serving it. Nevertheless, decanting is not simply allowing your wine to breathe, yet it is when you pour your wine inside a totally distinct container to enable the breathing. Certain individuals even use a special filter when decanting to get rid of bitter sediments which may have formed in the wine.

Younger wine bottles gain more from an aeration procedure than the older bottles. Nevertheless, the sediment is more prevalent with the older bottles. Plenty of individuals claim that airing out the bottle is able to relax the taste of the wine, making their taste more smooth. The wine may have better integration. Nevertheless, all wines do not gain from this technique. Certain wines are supposed to be drunk instantly after popping the cork from the bottle.

The ideal way to know if you have to allow a bottle of wine to air out or be decanted is to taste it initially. As quickly as you yank the cork off of the wine bottle, you can know by tasting if it has to air out a bit.

Blind Tasting

The ideal method to hold a wine tasting is by randomly offering the wine to your participants. This implies that you do not wish for the guests to recognize what you are offering them. You may wish to offer the wine in a black wine glass. Nevertheless, the guests ought to additionally not see the wine bottle shape, nor must they ever see the bottle label.

You never wish for a taster's judgment to be changed since they know particular details of a particular wine. Particular considerations which could change a taster's judgment regarding wine consist of the price, color, reputation, and the geographic region from which the wine.

Individuals have expectations regarding wine when they understand these considerations. In case a wine is really costly or stems from a specific geographical region, certain individuals have a tendency to have certain expectations. Getting rid of the expectations of the tasters makes it possible for a wine tasting to go better, and the wine scores are going to be more precise.

Vertical Tasting

During a vertical wine tasting, you are going to have one varietal of wine from the identical vintage. This implies you may have the identical wine from various years; 1998, 1999, 2000, and so on. The most frequent purpose of tasting wines such as this is to get a great idea of a specific wineries style and structure. You could additionally get a comprehension of how the various weather patterns impact grapes throughout specific years.

Horizontal Tasting

When a horizontal tasting happens, you are going to utilize the identical wine from several producers. This kind of tasting is going to enable you to identify which wineries you believe make better wine. This wine is going to be from the identical year and the identical kind of wine yet from various wineries.

Tasting Flights

During a tasting flight, you are going to have numerous wine glasses out for the tasters to test. Besides every wine glass, you are going to have a card, including the particulars of the wine, geographical demographics, winery, type, and more. Certain flights consist of as many as 40 wine glasses to be tasted.

This offers a taster a clue about what kinds of wines originated from specific portions of the world and more. You could additionally get an excellent grasp of the various tastes of the various kinds of wines when you taste wine during a flight.

Old and New World Tasting

Many individuals enjoy this kind of wine tasting. The Old World, based upon wine aficionados, is considered to be comprised of nations such as Italy, France, Spain, Austria, and so on. The New World is North America, South America, New Zealand, Australia and South Africa.

The reason these nations are seen as the New World is since they are brand-new to the wine-producing market and late starters. Nevertheless, these nations are notable in producing wines.

Plenty of individuals like to feature the identical kinds of wines from the old and brand-new worlds to ascertain which they enjoy more. Certain individuals like to use a vertical or horizontal technique with this additionally. There are lots of methods to vary it up so you could make your wine tasting prosperous.

Cheese and Wine Tasting

There are various palate influences which cheese has when you consume a specific wine. When you taste particular wine mixes effectively, you are going to comprehend how well wine and cheese actually do go together.

The ideal method to offer a Cabernet sauvignon is with blue cheese. All you require is simply a bit. You may offer the blue cheese with an unflavored French bread additionally. The blue cheese functions by covering the mouth and establishing a foundation which is going to soften the wine and make it taste great.

The ideal method to evaluate this is by taking a taste of the wine initially. Wait a moment. Then take a cheese bite and take one more drink. You are going to notice a huge distinction.

Wine and Chocolate Tasting

Wine and chocolate could go together if you pull it off properly. Certain individuals totally disagree, yet this is due to the fact that they do not know how to combine the two. When you consume wine with chocolate, it is necessary to be certain the wine is as sweet as the chocolate you are offering. In case you have a wine which is not as sweet as the chocolate, it is going to make the wine taste extremely sour.

If you wish to offer lighter wines during wine tasting with chocolate, it is ideal to stick to chocolates which are lighter as well. For example, the white chocolates are the ideal with lighter wines. White zinfandel is going to go extremely well when you match it with a chocolate which is bittersweet.

Priceless Tasting

Priceless wine tasting is not informing the attendees how much the wine bottle costs. If you have numerous wine bottles, you do not wish to let anybody know the wine cost. When people understand what the wine price is, their judgment is corrupted. Never disclose the wine price.

In case you think you need to tell the guests the wine price, make certain you tell them when the tasting is done. This is due to the fact that it is a natural understanding that a costly wine is better than a wine which costs a low dollar quantity of cash. This might hold true in certain scenarios, yet it isn't constantly the case. You do not want presumptions to be made before the wine has actually been tasted, or it is going to mess up the tasting.

Price Point Tasting

The price point tasting technique is really comparable to the priceless tasting. Nevertheless, you are going to utilize wines which are in the identical price range when you offer the wines. The crucial factor is to set up a baseline for the dollar quantity and adhere to it.

Big 8 Tasting

A Big 8 tasting consists of a wine tasting of the various varietals of the Big 8 wines in a tasting flight. The big 8 wines consist of white and red wines. The red wines featured in the Big 8 are Pinot Noir, Shiraz, Cabernet Sauvignon, and Merlot. The white wines featured in the Big 8 are the Riesling, Chardonnay, Sauvignon Blanc and Pinot.

This is a terrific method to have a wine tasting if your guests do not understand the distinctions with the various varietals. They could work their way through the wines and discover on their own the taste of each wine and the distinctions.

This is an enjoyable method to find out about wines. When you have newer wine tasters, this may be the initial kind of wine tasting you wish to have at home. In this manner, during the following wine tasting you have, your buddies are going to know what to anticipate with the various wine blends.

Chapter 7: How to Taste Wine

There is a correct technique to tasting wine. If you follow these actions, you are going to discover that you improve your basic understanding of wine and have a more prosperous wine tasting.

The initial thing you want to do is to take a look at the wine clarity and color. You are going to do this by pouring the wine in a glass and taking a look at it. Tilting the glass, you want to take a look at the wine color from the middle of the glass to the edges.

It is simpler to see the wine color in case there is a white background behind the wine glass. In case you are in a restaurant, you may wish to hold up a white tablecloth or a paper napkin.

When you evaluate the wine color, there are a couple of things to take a look at. If you are taking a look at red wine, is it purple, red, ruby, maroon, brick, garnet, or perhaps near to beige brown? White wine might seem pale yellow, golden, green, light brown, or amber, as well. The colors make a huge distinction.

As you take a look at the wine in your glass you additionally wish to see if there is any sediment. You are able to tell by swirling the glass. It is necessary to measure the wine opacity additionally. The wine might be watery looking, opaque, dark or clear. Is the wine dull in color or wonderfully shining? It might even be clear or cloudy. These elements are really crucial.

When you swirl a glass, it aids you to see numerous things. You could see if there is any sediment. It additionally assists by vaporizing a portion of the alcohol and releasing the natural aromas in the wine. This is going to assist you in acquiring a great impression of wine instantly. It is essential to find out how to effectively smell the wine.

Make certain to place your nose practically in the glass so you are able to inhale the wine. Consider what you smell. You may smell things such as flowers, berry, citrus, oak, and more.

Swirling the wine enables you to smell the true and natural wine aromas. The wine aroma is the most effective sign of the qualities of the wine that are distinct. You could additionally tell the wine quality by smelling it.

You are going to take a taste of the wine next. Drink the wine carefully and roll it around in your mouth. Think of the first impression of the wine on your palate. This is where integration can be found; alcohol material, tannin, residual sugars and acidity levels.

All of these ought to be balanced. You may discover one part has more than the other. There might not be a particular taste that you observe with the wine intensity. You are aiming to see if the wine is light, heavy, sweet, crisp, or dry.

Next you are going to actually taste the wine. This is referred to as the middle range stage. You are going to want to decide on the real taste profile. You may taste a spice or a fruit.

After tasting the wine you are going to additionally choose the length of time the taste stays in your mouth after swallowing. The aftertaste is really crucial. Certain extremely sweet tasting wines typically go bitter after a couple of seconds of tasting. This is where you truly are going to decide whether you like the wine or not.

Chapter 8: Hosting a Wine Tasting Celebration

Having a wine tasting celebration is a great deal of entertainment. Even though this may appear to be for just the classy crowd, anybody could learn more about wine. This is a fantastic method to get together and explore brand-new varietals. You could utilize any technique of wine tasting when you have a celebration.

The initial thing you want to do is identify the kind of wine tasting you wish to have with your buddies. The ideal 'first' wine tasting technique is the Big 8 since this provides everybody with an excellent idea of the distinctions of varietals right upfront. You can select from the vertical, horizontal, pairings with chocolate or cheese, or other techniques. It is up to you as it is your wine tasting celebration.

After that, you are going to want to determine who you will invite to the celebration. Make certain there is ample room for all of the visitors you wish to invite prior to sending out any invites. You need enough chairs for individuals to sit easily. You additionally do not wish to have way too many individuals as it may be a bad circumstance if individuals feel hurried.

When you consider the number of individuals you have at your wine tasting party, it is going to assist if you knew just how much wine you have to purchase. Make sure to have enough, so all of the people have the ability to taste identical wines.

Thinking of the 'who' in who you will invite is necessary additionally. You may not wish to invite buddies who believe they are experts on wine, or they may get a bit annoying. They additionally may take control of the whole learning procedure of the various wines. This should be enjoyable, so make certain to invite fun individuals and individuals who are open-minded.

You ought to create a card for every tasted wine. This is going to be filled out by every visitor as they taste every wine. They are going to have the ability to record the aroma they smell from every wine, the taste, what it tastes like with a particular cheese, and so on. You could additionally have them score the various wines on the rear of every card as well.

The ideal method to do a wine tasting with your buddies is by holding a blind wine tasting party. You are going to want dark-colored or black glasses so the guests can not see the colors of the various wines. By doing this, their perceptions are going to be more sincere and precise.

You additionally do not ever wish to tell your participants what the costs of a particular wine were since they are going to instantly pass judgment on whether or not it is an excellent wine. Certain individuals right away presume wine isn't good if it is cheaper than $100. Never tell the price to your participants, particularly if you have various wines differing considerably in price. It is fine to tell prices after the end of wine tasting.

It is essential to not have labels on the bottles or anyplace they could be discovered. In case you leave a label on the counter, then you might have a cheating guest. Enable the guests to use their senses correctly with no assistance or tips.

You do not need to go crazy when you decorate for a wine tasting party. It is essential to have a white table cloth so the wine color could be effectively evaluated. Many individuals like decorating with candles, flowers, and paintings. It is totally up to you how you wish to decorate at your celebration.

Make certain you have lot of light at your wine tasting party. This is essential or you are going to have trouble with appropriate assessments of the wine color. You may offer a really cloudy wine, yet if candle light is shining and the room is dim, it might appear brilliant.

When you offer wines at a wine tasting party, make certain that they are served from dry to sweet. Begin with the light white wines initially and work your way gradually to the heavy red and dark wines. You ought to additionally begin with younger wines to the older wines. In case you are performing a vertical test based upon years, then you are going to make certain to begin with the most recent wines initially.

When you pour wine at a wine tasting, make certain you pour sufficiently in the glass to taste the wine. 2 ounces is typically an ideal quantity to pour for your guests to get the correct quantity for a quality wine tasting.

Make certain to offer treats such as bread, and unsalted, unflavored crackers to your guests. You do not wish your guests to be starving. This is going to additionally cleanse their palate so they are prepared for the following wine to have a go at.

The most crucial factor to think about at a wine tasting party is driving. In case your wine tasting party includes individuals enjoying the wine and not simply tasting, then they are going to have to locate a ride home. Make certain rides have actually been organized so all of your guests are secure when the celebration is over.

Chapter 9: Offering Wine

Opening a Wine Bottle

When you open a wine bottle you may discover that it is hard in the beginning. You ought to end up being acquainted with the corkscrew you are utilizing prior to planting it in the cork. You do not want the cork to fall apart or wind up within the wine. This could be discouraging, particularly if there are small pieces in the wine that are difficult to pick out.

When you place a corkscrew in a wine bottle, make certain the end is right in the middle of the cork. Turn the corkscrew top up until the screw is nearly totally within the cork. As you turn the top handle you are going to see that the corkscrew sides are going to rise. You are going to push these 2 side handles down at the same time, and the cork is going to be removed from the bottle.

Temperature

Wine is ideal when it is offered at the appropriate temperature levels. Certain wines taste terrible if you offer them when they are too warm or perhaps too cooled. Certain wines are not supposed to be cooled but to be offered at room temperature level. You ought to understand what temperature levels are ideal, or you might destroy your wine tasting party with your buddies.

The ideal wine temperatures for offering wines at any time or at a wine tasting party are the following:

White Wines: Between 45 and 50 degrees

Rose Wines: Between 45 and 55 degrees

Sparkling Wines: Between 41 and 51 degrees

Fortified Wines: Between 54 and 65 degrees

Red wines: Between 50 and 64 degrees

Chilling Wine Properly

Lots of folks believe they are able to toss a wine bottle in the freezer for a couple of minutes, and it is completely cooled. The ideal technique of cooling a wine bottle is in an ice water bucket. You do not want simply a bucket loaded with ice.

Fill a bucket up nearly 3/4 full with ice. Then blend the bucket with water. Bury the bottle within this and enable it to chill for at least thirty minutes. When you chill wine in a fridge, it normally requires numerous hours to get to the appropriate temperature level.

You could create a bad wine if you leave it in the fridge too long additionally. You do not want to mess up an excellent wine bottle. When you choose you are prepared to consume it, make certain to place it on ice water. The wine and freezer do not blend well together, and you are not going to enjoy the wine taste.

Keeping Leftover Wine

When you keep remaining wine, make certain not to place it in the fridge since it is going to be sullied the following time you wish to consume it. Recork the wine and store it in a great location. The ideal method to keep wine bottles is by guaranteeing the cork stays damp, and by making sure that the wine is going to be at the lowest steady temperature as possible. You also want to make sure that there is no vibration in the storage area, and that it is not a storage location for other items which may smell lousy.

Something to bear in mind is that you must never ever buy those small mini wine racks and place them on top of your fridge. This is the ideal method to destroy a great wine bottle. It may look stylish in your kitchen area yet the heat of the fridge ruins the wine.

If you intend keeping the wine for an extended time period which might be longer than 6 months, then you ought to make certain that the storage location has high humidity, is dark, and has a low-temperature level. The perfect temperature levels are between 50 and 55 degrees, with 70 percent of humidity.

Indications of Oxidation

It may be actually awkward to offer a wine bottle to your buddies at a wine tasting celebration which is oxidized. You ought to take appropriate care of your wine, so you never ever have this issue. There are indications you are going to discover for oxidation.

These things consist of red wine discoloration to a brown tint. White wines are going to turn from white to golden yellow. The wine may smell odd and not how it ought to. The flavors may be extremely odd and unusual.

Tainted wine truly is messed up and undrinkable. It will not make you ill. However, it truly is intolerable to consume, and you will not wish to. During wine tasting, the ideal thing to do is purchase more than one wine bottle in case one of the bottles ends up being tainted. It takes place occasionally and often it isn't even your fault.

Conclusion

There are numerous factors to consider when it pertains to wine tasting with your buddies. Anybody can hold a wine tasting celebration. Tasting wine is not only for the fancy. It is a great deal of fun to find out more about wine and wine tasting.

Prior to holding a wine tasting party you ought to acquaint yourself with wine, the origin, and more. Discover the history of the various wines prior to offerin them to your buddies. It is going to be exciting for everybody to find out about various wines. Additionally, you want to understand how to taste the wine effectively. You do not simply take a sip of wine and provide your opinion on whether it tastes excellent or not. Make certain to offer it your finest wine evaluation you can.

Your wine tasting party is going to achieve success if you have down the correct etiquette and guidelines. Make certain to follow rules as these are unwritten guidelines and are seen as common sense to wine aficionados.

I hope that you enjoyed reading through this book and that you have found it useful. If you want to share your thoughts on this book, you can do so by leaving a review on the Amazon page. Have a great rest of the day.

Made in United States
North Haven, CT
19 October 2023

42892495R10039